Sue doesn't want to go to school today.

She stayed up late last night watching TV and didn't get her homework done. Her eyes are tired and she feels like a cold is starting.

This is going to be a bad day!

Your name _____

Draw a face showing how you feel today.

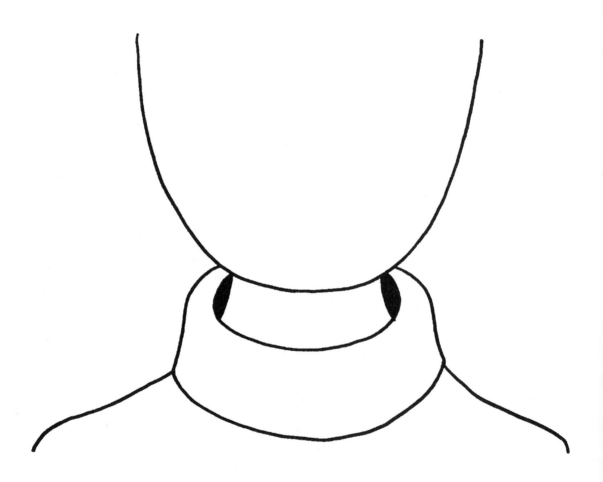

Artist: Brenda Brown   **Cover: Wilfred Spoon**
Copyright © James Boulden   Printed in USA
Boulden Publishing; P.O.Box 1186, Weaverville, CA 96093, Phone (800)238-8433

Sue looks out the window and sees her best friend, Nora, and the new girl next door walking to school together.

Sue can't believe her eyes. She and Nora always walk to school together.

How would you feel if you were Sue?

Nora and the new girl are talking like they are old friends. Nora points at Sue's house and they begin to giggle.

Sue feels hurt that the girls don't stop. She thinks Nora is talking about her and putting her down.

What would you do if you were Sue?

Sue starts to get angry.
She had trusted Nora as her best friend.
Now Nora and the new girl are laughing at her.
They must think Sue is stupid.

The more Sue thinks about it,
the madder she gets. Madder and madder.
Sue clinches her fists and stomps her feet.

What do you do when you are mad?

Color Sue mad.

HOW IT FEELS
TO BE MAD

1) Pay attention to your body.

2) Think of a time when someone made you really mad.

3) Think about what you would like to do or say to that person that made you mad.

(This is a chance for you to imagine all the mean and nasty things that you would be punished for doing in the real world.)

4) How do your hands feel now? _____

_____

5) Is your breathing faster or slower? _____

6) How do your jaws feel? _____

7) How do your cheeks feel? _____

8) Do you feel strong or weak? _____

9) Is your body relaxed or tense? _____

Remember these feelings the next time you begin to lose control. Then you can stop and choose what to do and say.

Sue feels her body shaking.
Her heart is beating fast and her face is hot.
She feels full of energy and wants
to hit something.

She slams the door on the way out
and shouts at Roger, her dog.

Why does Sue shout at Roger when he didn't do anything?

_____

_____

List two things that make you mad
and tell what you do about them.

WE ALL GET MAD SOMETIMES.

GRR!

MADMETER
- 0   →   10 -

1) _____

_____ makes me mad.

What I do about it is _____

_____

2) _____

_____ makes me mad.

What I do about it is _____

_____

Sue is late getting to school.
Then she talks back to the teacher when asked for her homework.

Why is Sue causing so much trouble?

_____

_____

Nora comes up to Sue
at recess and tries to be friendly.

Sue tells Nora to go away because
she doesn't like her anymore.

*Why doesn't Sue tell Nora
the real reason she is mad?*

Suddenly Sue is bumped
by John who is running to catch a ball.
John tells Sue he is sorry.

When John turns away, Sue throws the ball
and hits him hard on the head.

Why do you think Sue hit John with the ball?

Sue's friends come over to ask what's the matter.

Sue says Nora is really stupid and she isn't talking to her anymore.

What will happen when the girls tell Nora what Sue said?

_____

_____

Later that day, Sue is called into the principal's office for causing trouble between classes.

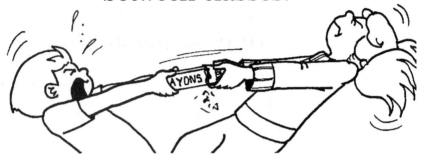

The principal tells Sue that she will have one day of lunch detention. Then he calls Sue's mom.

Why does Sue keep getting into more trouble?

_____

_____

That night Sue thinks about all the mean
things that people have done to her.
She feels the problems are not her fault.
The teacher gives too much homework
and Nora is stupid anyway.

Sue feels that she has a right to be mad.
It feels good to be angry.

*Describe a time when you felt like you were right
and everyone else was wrong.*

_____

_____

After awhile, Sue's anger turns to sadness.

She feels everyone is mad at her now.
Suddenly she starts to feel sick.

Why does Sue feel sad and sick?

_____

_____

Sue's mother hears crying and hurries to see what is wrong.

Sue is glad for someone to talk with. She tells her mom all the bad things that have happened this day.

Who can you talk with when you are upset?

Sue's mom says that it is OK to feel mad. Everyone gets mad at one time or another. The problems often come from what we do when we are mad. Sometimes we hurt other people and other times we hurt ourselves.

What is something you did or said when you were mad that you felt bad about later?

_____

_____

Mom helps Sue calm down.

Sue takes three deep breaths and counts to ten. Then she watches her breathing slow down. Sue can feel her body go limp like an old rag doll.

Why is it important for Sue to calm down before she does anything more?

SAFE WAYS TO HANDLE ANGER
Check those you will use.

☐ **Take time out and relax.**

Count to ten. Take three deep breaths. Feel rubbery.

☐ **Take a warm bath.**

Wash away the bad feelings.

☐ **Walk away from the problem.**

Go to a safe place where you can shout.

☐ **Run and play.**

Have some fun.

☐ **Put your feelings on paper. Draw and color.**

Make some angry pictures showing how you feel.

☐ **Hit something safe.**

Hit your pillow or kick a cushion.

☐ **Use humor. Make a joke out of it.**

See something funny in what happened. Laugh at yourself.

☐ **No big deal. Work with your mind.**

Decide if this problem is worth getting upset over.

☐ **Talk it out. Use "I" messages.**

Tell how you feel. Make a deal. Share. Ask them to stop.

☐ **Say you are sorry and make up.**

Only do this if you really mean it.

☐ **Get help from a grown-up.**

Or ask another kid to mediate.

Sue's mom tells her that the anger belongs to Sue. Sue can **choose** to stay mad or she can stop her anger.

Nobody is making Sue stay angry. She has to make a **choice**.

Check when is the best time to work out your anger:

❑ *Now?*
❑ *Tomorrow?*
❑ *Never?*

Sue's mom suggests that Sue tell Nora how she feels. It is phony for Sue to act like there is nothing wrong when there really is.

*Write a letter to someone who has hurt you
in the past and tell them how it made you feel.
Have an adult read the letter over with you.*

Dear _____

I felt _____

_____

when you _____

_____

because _____

_____

Signed _____

Sue goes right over to see Nora. She tells Nora how sad and disappointed she was that Nora didn't walk to school with her.

Nora says she is sorry. She was just trying to make the new girl feel welcome. The two girls go off to play together.

Why are kids sometimes afraid to say how they really feel when they are upset?

Sue can't watch television tonight because she has homework to do.

The next time Sue is mad, she is going to stop and think about what will happen if she causes trouble.

*What is the meaning of the word, **consequences**?*

Sue meets with her teacher before school the next day. Sue hands in the homework and says she is sorry that she talked back.

Sue and the teacher agree to talk about their problems next time. The teacher says it is important for Sue to respect other people.

How does the teacher feel about Sue now?

Sue knows she has caused a lot of trouble, and she has to try to put things right.

The next day Sue apologizes to John for hitting him with the ball.
She knows he didn't mean to bump her.

Why is it so hard to apologize?

John thanks Sue.
He says he has also done and said things when he was mad that he felt bad about later.

Write a letter to someone to whom you said or did something for which you are sorry.

Dear _____

Remember the time when _____

_____

I am sorry that I _____

_____

Something I learned from this is _____

_____

Signed _____

Sue has lots of time to think today
because she can't go out to recess.
All the other kids are playing and
she has to sit at her desk.

She decides that getting mad and causing
trouble just isn't worth all the problems
she has afterwards.

*Why is it important for Sue to make things right with the
people she has hurt?*

_____

_____

ANGER REPORT

Tell about the last time you were angry.

Why did you get mad?_____

_____

_____

Where did it happen? _____

_____

Who were you angry with?_____

_____

How mad did you get?_____

How long did you stay mad? _____

How did you handle it?_____

_____

Who did you tell about how you felt?_____

_____

What would you do differently next time? ___

_____

THINGS TO REMEMBER ABOUT ANGER

1. Everyone gets angry. You are not a bad person.
2. The anger is yours. You can choose not to be angry.
3. You may get mad over things that are not true.
4. The best time to stop anger is when it starts.
5. Problems are caused by how you act out your anger.
6. You may hurt yourself or others when you are mad.
7. It doesn't work to act like everything is OK when it isn't.
8. Anger often gets worse over time unless you stop it.
9. It is easy to get mad when you are tired or ill.

TIPS FOR MANAGING ANGER

1. Check your body to see how mad you are.
2. Stop and relax. Take deep breaths. Exercise.
3. Get away from the problem. Go to a safe place.
4. Realize that you have a choice in what you do.
5. Think of the different choices you have.
6. Think of the consequences of what you do.
7. Speak your feelings. Don't hold the anger inside.

THINGS YOU MAY BE SORRY FOR LATER

1. Hitting or kicking people or animals.
2. Causing trouble at school or home.
3. Saying things you don't mean.
4. Trying to get even.
5. Breaking things.

One thing about anger
is that it usually doesn't last very long.

Nora has invited Sue to her birthday party.
Today is a very happy day.

What is something you are happy about today?

ANGER SITUATIONS FOR DISCUSSION

Anger 1: Jonathan trips James in the hall. The other kids laugh when James falls to the floor. James gets up and starts hitting Jonathan.
    a. How do you think James feels after he falls?
    b. What could James do instead of hitting Jonathan?

Anger 2: Mr. Carzo, the teacher, gives Jenny homework that is too hard for her to do. Jenny shouts that it is too hard and runs out of the classroom.
    a. How do you think Jenny felt?
    b. What else could Jenny do?

Anger 3: Sue and Joan are playing in the yard at lunch. Joan hits Sue when Sue cheats at the game.
    a. Was Joan right to start a fight?
    b. What else could Joan have done?

CONTRIBUTING EDITORS TO THIS PUBLICATION

Fran Black, Rose Bomentre, Mary Bond, Russell Brown, Deb Bundy, P.A. Cotton, Audrey Dearborn, Steven Dolter, Delores Elms, Sheryl Frazier, Patricia Hauman, Lucy Holder, Dr. Karen Jamieson-Darr, Joann McCracken, Mary Anna Reimann, Dr. Anna Marie Resnikoff, Juanita Riley, John Rincker, Rachel Walker, Diane Way, Alice Wheaton, Linca Wilcox, Celeste Yaeger, Betti Ann Young.

ADDITIONAL RESOURCES FOR CHILDREN IN DISTRESS

Activity books, coloring books, reproducible workbooks, draw-a-face packs, games packs, videos, feelings posters & sweaters.

DIVORCE, BEREAVEMENT, SELF-ESTEEM, REMARRIAGE, BLENDED FAMILY, SINGLE PARENT, BULLY & VICTIM, FEELINGS, PARENTAL SUBSTANCE ABUSE, PHYSICAL & VERBAL ABUSE, SEXUAL ABUSE, AIDS, FAMILY ILLNESS, ANGER MANAGEMENT, CONFLICT RESOLUTION, COMMUNICATION.

Phone (800) 238-8433 for free brochure.
Boulden Publishing; P.O.Box 1186, Weaverville, CA 96093